Ferdinand Magellan

Alan Blackwood

Illustrations by Richard Hook

The Bookwright Press
New York · 1986

Great Lives

William Shakespeare
Queen Elizabeth II
Anne Frank
Martin Luther King, Jr.
Helen Keller
Ferdinand Magellan
Mother Teresa
John F. Kennedy

First published in the United States in 1986 by
The Bookwright Press
387 Park Avenue South
New York, NY 10016

First published in 1985 by
Wayland (Publishers) Limited
61 Western Road, Hove
East Sussex BN3 1JD, England

© Copyright 1985 Wayland (Publishers) Ltd

2nd impression 1986

Library of Congress Catalog Card Number: 85–71722

ISBN 0–531–18032–8

Phototypeset by Kalligraphics Ltd, Redhill, Surrey
Printed by G. Canale & C.S.p.A., Turin, Italy

Contents

Magellan's world

Every period of history has its own exciting record of achievements and events. The period we call the Renaissance – from about A.D. 1400 to 1600 – is remembered as a time of new ideas, inventions and discoveries. Shakespeare, Michelangelo, Leonardo da Vinci, Copernicus, Galileo, were some of the great people – writers and artists, scientists and thinkers – who made it such a golden age. Ferdinand Magellan, Portuguese navigator and explorer, was another.

Magellan, like most educated people in Renaissance Europe, had come to believe the world was round and shaped like a globe – not flat or saucer-shaped, as so many thought in those days. But neither he nor anyone else yet knew how big the world was, and could only guess at what vast and strange new lands might lie beyond the seas. To find out about these things was the greatest challenge of the age.

Portugal and Spain led the way in this great quest. In 1443, Henry the Navigator, a Portuguese prince, founded an observatory and school of navigation at Cape St. Vincent, a lonely headland jutting out into the Atlantic from the coast of Portugal. There, some of Europe's most learned astronomers and skilled map-makers devised new ways of charting the seas and continents. Later came the explorers themselves. Bartholomew Diaz and Vasco da Gama, in turn, charted the coast of Africa and sailed on eastward across the Indian Ocean. Christopher Columbus headed in the opposite direction, crossing the unknown Atlantic Ocean to reach the New World.

Not long after them, Magellan set sail on what was to prove the greatest voyage of discovery yet.

Opening up the trade routes

Ferdinand Magellan was tough and stocky, stubborn and brave – just the sort of man fitted for life at sea five hundred years ago.

He was born about the year 1480, and as a boy was sent to the court of the King and Queen of Portugal to become a page. He was taught music and dancing, but because King John of Portugal was interested in the sea, young Magellan and the other boys at court also had lessons in geography and

navigation.

He was excited, too, by the tales of daring Portuguese seamen, who sailed the Atlantic southward across the equator and round the southern end of Africa (soon to be named the Cape of Good Hope), so opening the way to new trade routes to the East.

Magellan was nineteen when, in 1499, Vasco da Gama sailed back into Lisbon harbor with a cargo of silks, pearls, opium and spices from India. By taking the route around Africa and across the Indian Ocean, he had also just completed the longest sea voyage up to that time.

Magellan longed to go to sea himself, but luck, for the

Henry the Navigator planning his voyages at his observatory at Cape St. Vincent.

Many expeditions set sail from the busy quayside at Lisbon, in the 14th and 15th centuries.

moment, was against him. King John was murdered, and was succeeded by his brother-in-law, Duke Manuel. The new king showed much less interest in sea exploration. He also seems to have disliked Magellan. For six years King Manuel refused or ignored all young Magellan's pleas to be allowed to leave the court and become a sailor.

To sea at last

Though he cared little about the sea and ships, King Manuel was interested in riches and power. The world trade in pepper and other spices was very important in this respect. In the centuries before refrigeration, spices were widely used for preserving food. For many years, Arab traders had grown rich, bringing spices to Europe from the East, by way of the Arabian Sea and Africa.

King Manuel now commissioned an armada of twenty-two fighting ships to chase away the Arab traders from the African coast and the surrounding seas. This left the way open for Portuguese traders to bring pepper, cloves and nutmeg to Europe by the new sea routes to and from the East.

This was Magellan's chance. He asked again for leave of absence from the court, in order to join the armada. This time the king agreed, and in 1505, Magellan, age twenty-five, went to sea.

Magellan was put in charge of a swift-moving galley and he and his crew sank many Arab craft along the coast of East Africa. He

Portuguese merchant ships put to sea.

was wounded while helping to defeat a large Arab fleet near the port of Diu in northwest India.

But Magellan was more interested in exploration than fighting. The king rewarded him with the command of a ship and he joined a Portuguese expedition sailing down the Malacca Strait between Sumatra and Malaya and on to the fabled Spice Islands (now part of Indonesia).

From there, he set course across what one chronicler called "seas no Christian man has yet entered into." At the very limit of the then known world, he discovered parts of the Philippine Islands.

Instead of returning to honor and fame in Portugal, Magellan, after six years at sea, found himself in great trouble.

Disgrace

The cause of Magellan's trouble was the Treaty of Tordesillas of 1494. This was an agreement between Portugal and Spain to share the newly discovered regions of the world between them. The division ran north to south down a line west of the mid-Atlantic Ocean and through part of Brazil. Spain claimed all new seas and lands west of this imaginary line. Regions to the east of the line would belong to Portugal.

The question still to be decided was how far did these areas extend around the far side of the globe.

When he discovered the Philippines, Magellan was unwise enough to suggest that they were so far around to the east of the globe that they might come within the Spanish half of the world.

King Manuel of Portugal was outraged. Despite the treaty, Spain was still a rival. Magellan, for all his proven bravery and skill as a sailor, was therefore in deep disgrace.

A 16th century view of Lisbon, chief port and capital of Portugal.

The King dismissed all Magellan's entreaties for another ship.

In 1513, Magellan was wounded again, fighting against the Moors in North Africa. This injury caused him to walk with a limp for the rest of his life. Back home, he pleaded with King Manuel to give him command of another ship, but the monarch called him "club foot" and dismissed all his entreaties.

The one bright spot in this miserable period of Magellan's life was his friendship with another great Portuguese navigator, John of Lisbon. John shared the opinion, held by many seamen and explorers of the time, that the Far East and the Spice Islands could also be reached by sailing westward around the world. This belief had inspired Columbus's famous voyage of 1492. John had followed Columbus across the Atlantic and then explored the coast of South America. He thought he had found the point where the coast swung westward, so offering a way round for shipping.

Magellan longed for a chance to find a way around the South American continent.

Two exciting years

Magellan's chance came in 1517. Because of his reputation as a skilled and fearless sailor, he was invited to Seville in neighboring Spain. There he met Duarte Barbosa, a successful Portuguese captain who lived in Spain. Plans were made for an expedition, to be commanded by Magellan, to find John of Lisbon's South American passage to the Far East – "El Paso." The King of Spain, Charles I, gave the expedition his blessing and financiers put up the money. At this time, Magellan married Barbosa's daughter Beatrice, who bore him a son.

Magellan took charge of all the preparations for the voyage – recruiting the crews, ordering and checking supplies of food, spare canvas, masts and rigging, guns and other arms. King Manuel sent spies to report on the preparations and to make mischief, and the merchants and bankers financing the enterprise also interfered. But by the late summer of 1519, the expedition was ready to sail.

There were five ships in the expedition. We have no detailed records of them, but they were probably early types of galleon. The largest, the *San Antonio*, was about 48 meters (150 feet) in length. The others, in order of size, were the *Trinidad, Victoria, Concepcion* and *Santiago*.

Such ships look very attractive in pictures, but they were no fun to sail in. They were cramped and crowded, with little room for rest and shelter, and they were infested with lice and rats.

Food and drink was another big problem on board. Salted meat, cheese, biscuits, water and

Magellan's ship, the Victoria.

wine were the main provisions. This was a poor diet at the best of times. Often, the food went rotten and the wine and water turned sour, so that there was nothing fit to eat or drink.

Diseases like typhoid and dysentery, and a terrible sickness called scurvy, killed many sailors in those days.

The voyage begins

At last the expedition set sail, on September 20, 1519. It reached Tenerife, one of the Canary Islands, seven days later. Here there were the first signs of conflict and disagreement between Magellan, as Captain-General of the fleet, and the Spanish captains in charge of individual ships.

The main cause of the dispute was that Magellan was a true explorer, anxious to discover more about the world, while his captains were interested only in finding a new and profitable trade route to the Spice Islands. In addition, because of the rivalry between Portugal and Spain, Magellan and his captains did not trust each other.

Matters came to a head when they started arguing about the course they should follow across the Atlantic. One of the captains, Juan de Cartagena, tried to organize a revolt. Magellan had him arrested and put in chains. For the moment he had restored law and order.

Becalmed

As the fleet sailed on, it ran into violent thunderstorms. These created a strange effect, known to sailors as St. Elmo's Fire. Masts glowed and flickered with a ghostly light. This is caused by electricity in the atmosphere, but in those days sailors knew nothing of electricity and they believed the light meant that St. Elmo, patron saint of seamen, was protecting them.

Then they drifted into the doldrums, a region of almost windless calm near the equator.

For three weeks the ships were becalmed under the blazing sun.

For over three weeks Magellan's ships lay becalmed, while the sun blazed down. Tar melted in the timbers, causing the ships to spring leaks. Water and wine casks burst and food went rotten.

Fortunately, ocean currents slowly carried the ships across the doldrums, until at last they began to pick up the brisk northeast trade winds. The ships' sails filled again, and they were back on course, heading for the South American continent.

Hopes dashed

The expedition arrived off the coast of South America early in December 1519. This is summertime in countries south of the equator. They anchored in the bay of what is now Rio de Janeiro, near the beautiful Sugar Loaf mountain. The crews carried out repairs, took aboard fresh food and water, and made friends with the local Indians. Magellan always made friendly approaches toward the people of the countries he visited – unlike most explorers of the time, who were bent only on conquest and possession.

He was also full of hope, when they got under way again, on Christmas day. Although most of South America was still unknown, geographers estimated that the continent was about the same size and shape as Africa, and that it occupied about the same position north and south of the equator. If this were so, then Magellan was well on the way to finding a passage round the southern end of South America.

Geographers also believed that another large land mass existed even farther south, which they

An early map of southern South America.

called *Terra Australis Incognita* (the Unknown Southern Land) and Magellan hoped to find it.

In January 1520, sailing southward, the fleet reached a point where the coast did indeed swing round to the west as far as the eye could see – just as John of Lisbon had described it. This, thought Magellan, must be "El Paso." He dispatched the *Santiago* to follow the coast around, while he sailed on with the others, sure also that he would soon locate *Terra Australis*.

The truth came as a bitter disappointment. What appeared to be "El Paso" was just one side of the very wide estuary of the River Plate. On the far side of the estuary, the coast continued southward, where *Terra Australis* ought to have

Mutiny

Such a setback only made Magellan more determined than ever to find a way around, or through, the South American continent. So, after a further rest, the expedition proceeded south again, sailing into some of the stormiest seas in the world. The wind was sometimes so strong it actually blew them backward. Ice formed on masts and rigging, making the ships top-heavy, and even more likely to capsize in the raging seas.

With only such simple instruments as hourglass and compass, Magellan nevertheless held his wooden galleons to their course for more than 1500 kilometers (over 1000 miles) down the rugged coast of what is now Argentina. Only when his crews were dropping from cold and exhaustion did he finally seek shelter, in the natural

harbor of San Julian.

By now the expedition was well into uncharted regions and had reached one of the loneliest places on earth, at almost the coldest time of the year. Here, three of Magellan's Spanish captains mutinied, planning to sail their ships, the *San Antonio, Victoria* and *Concepcion*, back home to Spain as soon as the weather allowed.

Although exhausted after weeks with hardly any sleep and little food, Magellan acted swiftly.

An hourglass used for navigation.

A traverse board with string and pegs, used by seamen to plot a course.

With the two remaining ships (the *Trinidad* and *Santiago*) still loyal to him, he immediately blockaded the harbor entrance. Then, with his knowledge of tides and currents, he outmaneuvered the other three ships, recapturing each in turn. In the process, one of the captains, Luis de Mendoza, was stabbed to death. A second captain, Gaspar de Quesada, was afterward put on trial and executed. Mutinous crew members were condemned to work in chains. Magellan was in command again.

19

Land of the big feet

Magellan and his crew saw penguins on the coast of Patagonia.

We know many details of Magellan's epic voyage, thanks to Antonio Pigafetta, an Italian who joined the expedition as chronicler, or reporter. He has left us a vivid account of winter at San Julian.

There were, he reports, enough trees to provide timber for the construction of log cabins. These housed the crews while they cleaned and repaired the battered ships. Pigafetta also describes the wildlife, writing of "goslings that are black and white and do not fly," and "sea wolves with large teeth and no legs." These were penguins and seals, the first ever to be seen by white men. The animals provided the members of the expedition with fresh meat, oil for lamps and skins for extra winter clothing.

Most fascinating of all is Pigafetta's account of a race of giants, after whom the region takes its name of Patagonia – "Land of the Big Feet." "One day," he records, "we saw on the shore a huge giant, completely naked, who danced, leaped and sang, all the while throwing sand and dust over his head. He was so tall that even the largest of us came only midway between his waist and his shoulder." Fifty-seven years later, Sir Francis Drake, exploring the same stretch of coast, also reported seeing men well over 2 meters (7 feet) tall.

What has since happened to this race of giant people is a mystery. But according to Pigafetta, Magellan first made friends with them. He then made the mistake of trying to capture two of the giants to take back with him to Spain. There was a fight, during which one of his crew was killed, and the giants got away. Magellan, having lost their trust, was afraid they might attack the expedition. That was why, despite the terrible winter weather, he gave orders to sail on.

"El Paso" found

The expedition found new winter quarters in the estuary of the Santa Cruz River. However, the *Santiago*, smallest of the ships, was stranded on a sand bank, where all but one of her crew just managed to jump to safety before she was smashed to pieces.

In October 1520, the expedition put to sea again. It was springtime, but they were now closer to the South Pole than any men or ships before them, in seas where storms can blow up at any time of the year.

They found this out when winds of hurricane force struck suddenly. Magellan's flagship, the *Trinidad*, and the *Victoria*, managed to ride out the storm, though the wind ripped sails to shreds and snapped off masts, and mountainous waves swept men overboard. The other two vessels, the *San Antonio* and *Concepcion*, were driven helplessly toward a line of jagged rocks on one side of a horseshoe-shaped bay. There seemed no hope for them.

They had discovered "El Paso."

When the storm abated, Magellan moved the *Trinidad* in close to land, vainly scanning rocks and shore for any sign of wreckage or survivors. Suddenly his look-out cried "A sail! I see a sail!" Coming round the bay were the *San Antonio* and *Concepcion*, sails billowing, pennants proudly flying. Wind and waves had carried them past the rocks and into a deep-water channel that ran almost due west toward distant cliffs and mountains. Their crews knew it was not the entrance to another river, by observing the tides and by testing the saltiness of the water. It was a seawater strait. Magellan realized they had found "El Paso" at last.

The biggest ocean

Magellan led his ships through the deep and narrow strait which is now named after him. During this difficult exercise in navigation, the captain and crew of the *San Antonio* managed what they had failed to do at San Julian — they slipped away and headed back to Spain. Undaunted, Magellan and his three remaining ships entered the "Great South Sea." He called his men together for a service of thanksgiving, and solemnly named it the *Mar Pacifico* ("Peaceful Sea").

Magellan reckoned it was now only a matter of days before the expedition reached the Philippines or Spice Islands. He eagerly plotted their westerly course across the blue Pacific,

The bleak landscape of Tierra del Fuego near the Straits of Magellan.

aided once more by the brisk trade winds. But, as day followed day, then week followed week, with no sight or sign of land, the crews became anxious and restive. Magellan himself realized something was very wrong with his calculations. His "sea" was, in fact, the biggest ocean of all, covering a third of the total surface of the world.

The voyage proved a terrible ordeal. In all that vast and empty ocean, they came upon just one tiny, uninhabited island. Stocks of food and water ran low. Worse still, as they sailed back into the tropics, what little food was left went rotten. The men ate anything they could find, rats, maggots, strips of leather, even sawdust. They began to suffer from scurvy. Their skin broke out in sores, their limbs became horribly swollen, they grew so weak they could not stand or even raise an arm. One by one they died.

When the expedition finally reached the Mariana Islands, some 2,000 kilometers (1,250 miles) east of the Philippines, the survivors had crossed nearly 13,000 kilometers (over 8,000 miles) of the Pacific Ocean.

The Philippines

The natives of the Marianas were a warlike race, armed with clubs, spears and shields decorated with the hair of people they had killed. Magellan and his men, starving and sick, had to fight them off with crossbows and cannon fire. They made a quick landing, grabbed what food and drink they could find, and put to sea again.

Ten days later they reached the Philippines, where, thankfully, the situation was very different. The small island of Homonhon, where they first landed, was a beautiful place of sandy beaches, palm trees and abundant fish, fruit and vegetables. There they rested and recovered their health and strength. The local Filipinos were very friendly, loading their visitors with more food, and with pearls, gold and precious stones, in exchange for such items as knives and mirrors.

For Magellan himself, it was a tremendous personal triumph. Years before, he had first reached the Philippines by sailing east from Portugal. Now he had returned, by sailing westward.

Taking the two voyages together, he was thus the first man to have been right around the world.

More triumphs seemed to be in store for him when the *Trinidad, Concepcion* and *Victoria*, escorted by islanders in hundreds of canoes, moved on to the neighboring island of Cebu. The king or rajah of Cebu was converted to Christianity. Magellan ordered a large cross to be erected on the shore, and an altar to be built. The rajah and thousands of his subjects, were then baptized by the ships' priests. With this ceremony,

Magellan's Cross on Cebu today.

Magellan claimed the Philippines for Christendom and for Spain.

If Magellan had returned to Spain, he would surely have received a hero's welcome. But he did not return.

A tragic end

Magellan became obsessed with converting more Filipinos to Christianity. With this aim in mind, on April 27, 1521, he and a small band of volunteers landed on an island across the water from Cebu. But instead of being welcomed, they were attacked by the islanders. Because of his limp, Magellan could not defend himself very well. He was driven back into the water and killed with clubs and arrows.

It was a tragic end for the man who had led one of the most heroic of all voyages of discovery. He had charted over 2,000 kilometers (1,243 miles) of the coast of South America, discovered and crossed the Pacific Ocean, and proved beyond all doubt that the world was round.

The last leg

Magellan's old enemies, the Spanish officers, were glad that their leader was dead. Now they could proceed to the Spice Islands without further delay.

They burnt Magellan's log books, hoping to destroy all record of the mutiny and other quarrels. Then they scuttled the *Concepcion*, because there were not enough fit men left to sail her. When they reached the Spice Islands, they were so greedy that they overloaded the *Trinidad* with spices, silks and gold, and she sank.

Only the *Victoria*, commanded by Sebastian del Cano, completed the long voyage westward across the Indian Ocean, around the coast of Africa, and so back to Spain.

On September 6, 1522, she dropped anchor off the mouth of the Guadalquivir River. Out of the original company of 277 who had set sail from that same point three years earlier, only 18 had returned – the first men actually to circumnavigate the world.

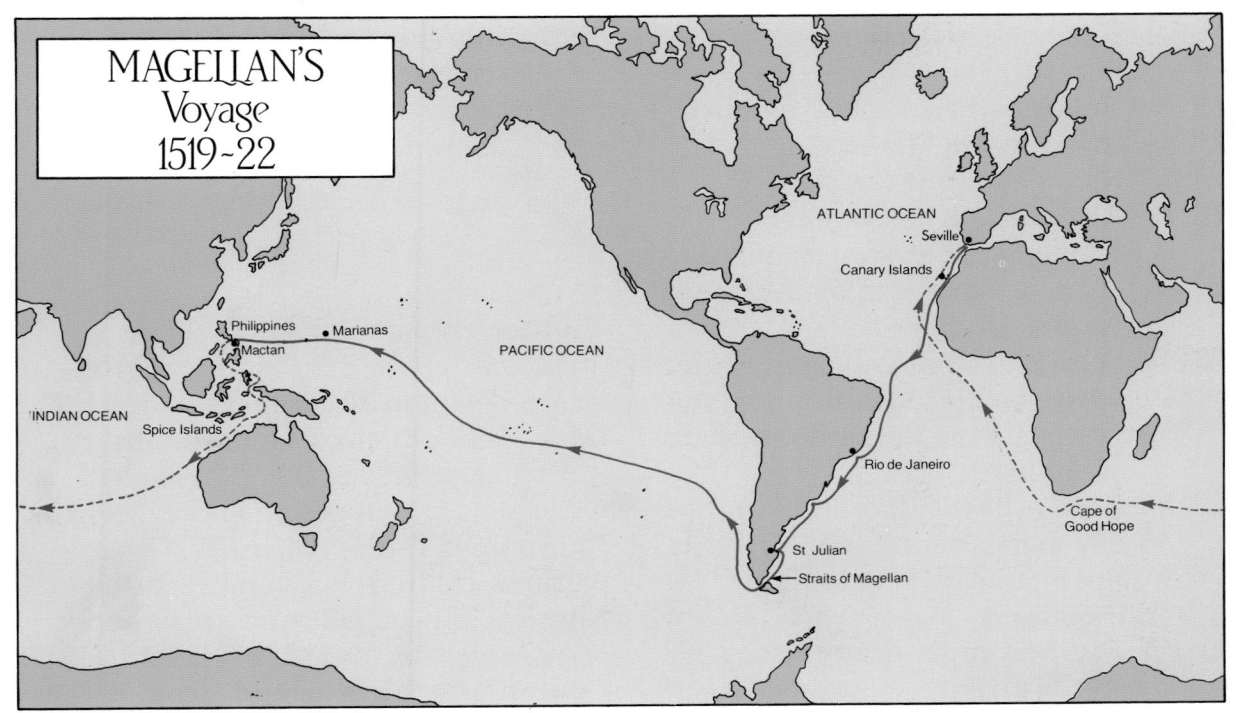

MAGELLAN'S
Voyage
1519~22

Dates and events

1480 Birth of Ferdinand Magellan in Oporto, Portugal.

1492 Becomes an apprentice page at the court of the King and Queen of Portugal.

1494 Treaty of Tordesillas between Portugal and Spain divides the world in half, between the two countries.

1505 Magellan goes to sea for the first time, on an expedition to the Indian Ocean. Is seriously wounded in a sea battle with Arab traders.

1512 Discovers the Philippines. Suggests they might lie in Spain's half of the world, and is sent back to Portugal in disgrace.

1513 Volunteers for service against the Moors in Morocco. Is wounded in the leg.

1516 Appeals to King Manuel of Portugal to be given command of an expedition to the East, but is refused.

1517 Is invited to neighboring Spain, where he presents his plan for a voyage to the Pacific to the King of Spain.

1519 *Sept*. A fleet of five ships and 277 men set sail from Seville in Spain, under Magellan's command.
Dec. The ships enter the bay of Rio de Janeiro.

1520 *Jan*. Magellan believes he has found "El Paso," but this proves to be the estuary of the River Plate.
Aug. Crushes mutiny at Port St. Julian.
Oct. The *San Antonio* and *Concepcion* are blown off course and "El Paso" is found.
Nov. The fleet sails through the straits and enters the Pacific Ocean.

1521 *March* Ships reach the Mariana Islands.
April Ships arrive at the Philippines. Magellan is killed on the island of Mactan.

1522 One ship and eighteen men return to Seville – completion of the first circumnavigation of the world.

Picture credits

Glossary

Armada A great fleet of ships, armed for war.

Astronomers Scientists who study the stars and planets.

Circumnavigate To travel right around the world.

Compass An instrument for finding direction. It has a magnetized needle that points toward the magnetic north pole.

Doldrums Stretches of ocean near the equator, where there is almost no wind and the sea is dead calm.

Equator An imaginary line encircling the Earth midway between the north and south poles, and dividing the world into the northern and southern hemispheres.

Financiers Bankers or people who lend money.

Galleon A large sailing ship, which was used as a trader or warship from the 15th to the 18th centuries.

Galley A type of ship propelled mainly by oars, but often using sails as well.

Hourglass An instrument for measuring hours by the running of sand from one glass container into another through a narrow opening. It takes exactly one hour for the sand to run through.

Log book The official, day-to-day record of a ship's voyage, kept by the captain or other commanding officer.

Mutiny A rebellion by seamen against their officers.

Scurvy A disease caused by lack of vitamin C, which is found in fresh fruit and vegetables.

Scuttle To deliberately sink a ship by opening the sea cocks, or making holes in its bottom.

Trade winds Winds that blow steadily toward the equator.

Books to read

Bitossi, Sergio. *Ferdinand Magellan*. Morristown, NJ: Silver Burdett, 1984.

Brownlee, Walter. *The First Ships Round the World*. New York: Cambridge University Press, 1974.

Grosseck, Joyce. *Great Explorers*, revised edition. Grand Rapids, MI: Fideler Co., 1981.

Harley, Ruth. *Ferdinand Magellan*. Mahwah, NJ: Troll Associates, 1979.

Ross, Stewart. *Columbus and the Age of Exploration*. New York: Franklin Watts/Bookwright, 1985.

Sandak, Cass R. *Explorers and Discovery*. New York: Franklin Watts, 1983.

Syme, Ronald. *Magellan: First Around the World*. New York: Morrow, 1953.

Wilkie, Katherine. *Ferdinand Magellan: Noble Captain*. Boston: Houghton Mifflin, 1963.

Index